CANADA

CANADA

Collins

Contents

Introduction

"Canada is like an expanding flower—wherever you look you see some fresh petal unrolling." —Sir Arthur Conan Doyle, 1914

Canada, full of natural splendour, is home to some of the world's most incredible mountains, cities, and wilderness areas, and has the longest coastline in the world. A paradise for explorers and photographers, Canada offers endless opportunities to find beauty: from the majesty of the Rocky Mountains to the breadth of the sweeping Prairies to the wonder of the rising sun over the Atlantic Ocean. But the magic of Canada is also found in fishing at one of Canada's many freshwater lakes, discovering the vibrancy of its cities, marvelling at stunning fall colours, and spotting mountain goats snuggling on a snowy ledge.

Bringing together over 250 spectacular images from award-winning photographers for you to explore and enjoy, *Canada* takes you across 5,514 km, from Cape Spear, Newfoundland and Labrador, to Mount Saint Elias in the Yukon, from sea to sea.

British Columbia

ABOVE: Marble Canyon, Kootenay National Park

RIGHT: Kicking Horse River, Yoho National Park

Jumbo Pass in the Purcell Mountains, near Golden

ABOVE: Orcas in Johnstone Strait

LEFT: Stanley Park Seawall and Vancouver skyline

ABOVE: Snowboarder in Whistler

RIGHT: Mount Burgess over Emerald Lake Lodge, Yoho National Park

Surfer at Chesterman Beach, Tofino, Vancouver Island

ABOVE: Haffner Creek Falls, Kootenay National Park

LEFT: Black bear cubs in Mount Revelstoke National Park

ABOVE: Khutzeymateen Inlet, Khutzeymateen Grizzly Bear Sanctuary

RIGHT: Salmon spawning upstream off of Princess Royal Island

Royal Canadian Mounted Police in Langley

ABOVE: Vineyards along Okanagan Lake

RIGHT: Mount Assiniboine Provincial Park

ABOVE: Grey wolf in Golden

RIGHT: Humpback whale in Johnstone Strait

Aerial view of Vancouver

ABOVE: British Columbia Parliament Buildings, Victoria, Vancouver Island

LEFT: Chinatown, Victoria, Vancouver Island

Wildflower meadow in the Selkirk Mountains

ABOVE & LEFT: Khutzeymateen Grizzly Bear Sanctuary, near Prince Rupert

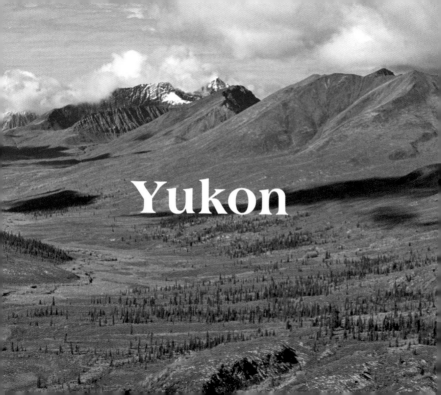

Yukon

ABOVE: Glacial pools at Kaskawulsh Glacier, Saint Elias Mountains

RIGHT: Saint Elias Mountains, Kluane National Park and Reserve

Tombstone Territorial Park

ABOVE: The SS *Klondike*, Yukon River, Whitehorse

LEFT: Hubcap totem poles in Champagne

Dawson City

41

Dogsledding in the Yukon

Northern lights over Whitehorse

ABOVE: Abandoned Venus mine tailing site

RIGHT: Grizzly bears along the Alaska Highway

Kluane National Park and Reserve

ABOVE: Cow moose and calves near the Alaska Highway

RIGHT: North Fork Klondike River Valley, Tombstone Territorial Park

ABOVE: Cross-country skier in the Yukon

LEFT: Resting atop a Yukon mountain range

Alberta

ABOVE: Peyto Lake, Banff National Park

RIGHT: Trans-Canada Highway near Calgary

Prince of Wales Hotel, Waterton Lakes National Park

ABOVE: Moraine Lake Road, Banff National Park

RIGHT: Camping at Moraine Lake, Banff National Park

ABOVE: North Saskatchewan River, Edmonton

RIGHT: Bow River, Calgary

ABOVE: Downtown Jasper

RIGHT: Cattle drive near Calgary

Mount Rundle, Banff National Park

ABOVE: Lake Minnewanka, Banff National Park

RIGHT: Morant's Curve, Canadian Pacific Railway, Bow Valley Parkway

ABOVE: Canada lynx in Banff National Park

RIGHT: Mountain goat nanny and kid in Jasper National Park

70

Lake Minnewanka, Banff National Park

ABOVE: Dinosaur Provincial Park, Canadian Badlands

RIGHT: Castle Mountain and the Bow River, Banff National Park

ABOVE: Bighorn rams above Talbot Lake, Jasper National Park

LEFT: Head-Smashed-In Buffalo Jump World Heritage Site

ABOVE: Male elk in Banff National Park

RIGHT: Herd of cow elk on the David Thompson Highway

ABOVE: Aspen stand in Banff National Park

RIGHT: Chateau Lake Louise, Banff National Park

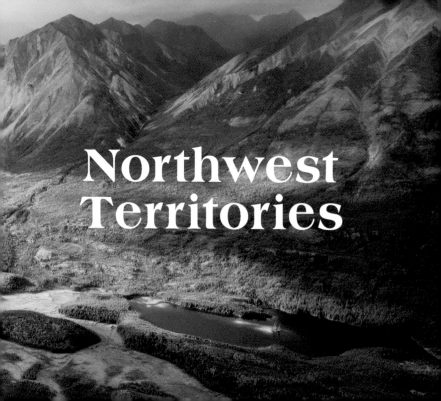

Northwest
Territories

Vale Island, Hay River

ABOVE: Oil detection site near Lougheed Island

RIGHT: Death Lake, Nahanni National Park Reserve

ABOVE: Cargo plane at the Kennady Diamonds' Kelvin Camp in Yellowknife

RIGHT: Herd of bull muskoxen on Banks Island

ABOVE: Yellowknife

LEFT: Sun dog optical phenomenon on Great Slave Lake, Yellowknife

Dettah Ice Road, Great Slave Lake

ABOVE: Vuntut National Park

RIGHT: Wood bison

ABOVE: Yellowknife Bay, Great Slave Lake

RIGHT: Alexandra Falls, Hay River

Deh Cho Bridge, Mackenzie River

ABOVE: Ice hockey in Yellowknife

LEFT: Ice fishing in Great Slave Lake, Yellowknife

Cirque of the Unclimbables, Nahanni National Park Reserve

ABOVE: Grasslands National Park

RIGHT: Trans-Canada Highway near Moosejaw

Hanley

ABOVE: Pierceland

LEFT: Pumpjack near Carlyle

St. John the Baptist Ukrainian Catholic Church
in the ghost town of Smuts

ABOVE: Limerick

RIGHT: Kenaston

ABOVE: Wild burrowing owl chicks

LEFT: Avonhurst

Great Sandhills Ecological Reserve

ABOVE: Golden wheat field

RIGHT: Pronghorns in southeastern Saskatchewan

First Nations University of Canada, Regina

ABOVE: South Saskatchewan River, Saskatoon

RIGHT: Walter Scott Memorial and Saskatchewan Legislative Building, Regina

Broadway and Victoria Bridges, Meewasin Valley, Saskatoon

ABOVE: Cunningham River, Somerset Island

RIGHT: Arctic foxes on Somerset Island

ABOVE: Devon Island

LEFT: Auks flying by Somerset Island

Apex, Iqaluit

ABOVE: Expedition camp at Bylot Island, Baffin Bay

RIGHT: Iceberg near Bylot Island, Baffin Bay

ABOVE: Sirmilik National Park

LEFT: Sam Ford Fjord, Baffin Island

Sam Ford Fjord, Baffin Island

ABOVE: Pangnirtung

RIGHT: Iqaluit International Airport Terminal

ABOVE: Barren-ground caribou

RIGHT: Iceberg near Qikiqtarjuaq Village, Baffin Island

Walrus mother and calf in Lancaster Sound

ABOVE: Narwhal north of Baffin Island

RIGHT: Beluga whale pod off of Port Leopold, Somerset Island

ABOVE & RIGHT: Polar bears in Lancaster Sound

ABOVE: Canadian Coast Guard ship in Bellot Strait

RIGHT: Polar bear in Tremblay Sound

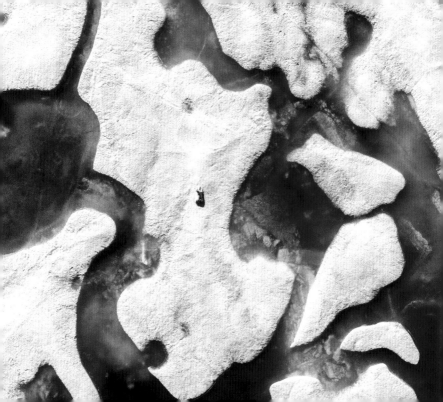

Northern lights over Ennadai Lake

ABOVE: Sunset Beach, Lake Winnipeg

LEFT: Teepee in Churchill

ABOVE & RIGHT: Canadian Museum for Human Rights, Winnipeg

Provencher Bridge across the Red River, Winnipeg

163

ABOVE: Manitoba Legislative Building and Louis Riel statue, Winnipeg

RIGHT: Royal Canadian Mint, Winnipeg

164

ABOVE: Manitoba Legislative Building, Winnipeg

RIGHT: Grain elevator in Carey

Campers Cove, Clearwater Lake Provincial Park

ABOVE: Beluga whales in Churchill River, Hudson Bay

RIGHT: Polar bear and Tundra Buggy in Churchill

ABOVE: Totem pole in St. Vital Park, Winnipeg

LEFT: Northern lights in The Pas

ABOVE: Ice fishing hut on the Red River, near Winnipeg

RIGHT: Arctic fox on the frozen coast of Hudson Bay, near Churchill

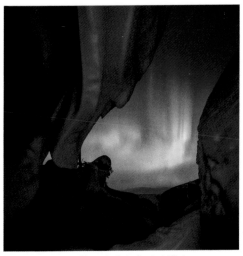

ABOVE: The caves at Clearwater Lake Provincial Park

RIGHT: Northern lights in Churchill

Ontario

ABOVE: Lake of Bays, Muskoka

LEFT: Dorset, Muskoka

ABOVE: Point Pelee National Park

RIGHT: View from the Top of the Giant, Lake Superior, Thunder Bay

ABOVE: Wood duck drake in Ottawa

LEFT: Costello Lake, Algonquin Provincial Park

ABOVE: Indian Falls, Owen Sound

RIGHT: Horseshoe Falls, Niagara Falls

ABOVE: *Maman* by Louise Bourgeois, National Gallery of Canada, Ottawa

RIGHT: Peace Tower, Parliament Hill, Ottawa

ABOVE: Rideau Canal Skateway, Ottawa

RIGHT: Central Chambers, Ottawa

Mizzy Lake Trail, Algonquin Provincial Park

ABOVE: Centre Island, Toronto

RIGHT: Cherry blossoms in High Park, Toronto

Toronto skyline

ABOVE: Rower at Sunnyside Beach on Lake Ontario, Toronto

RIGHT: Fu Yao Supermarket, East Chinatown, Toronto

ABOVE: Gooderham Building, Toronto

LEFT: Aga Khan Museum, Toronto

Michael Lee-Chin Crystal,
Royal Ontario Museum, Toronto

Quebec

ABOVE: Bonhomme, Quebec Winter Carnival

RIGHT: Quebec City

ABOVE: Rue du Cul-de-Sac, Quebec City

LEFT: Petit-Champlain District, Quebec City

ABOVE: Île aux Lièvres, St. Lawrence River

RIGHT: White-tailed deer in Omega Park, Montebello

Bonaventure Island

ABOVE: Mont-Saint-Bruno National Park

LEFT: Devil's River, Mont-Tremblant National Park

ABOVE: Rivière-au-Renard, Gaspé

RIGHT: Ungava Bay

ABOVE: Magdalen Islands

LEFT: Port-au-Persil

ABOVE: Common loon in northern Quebec

RIGHT: Maple syrup tapping

ABOVE: The Basilica of Saint-Anne-de-Beaupré, Quebec City

LEFT: Interior of the Notre Dame Basilica, Quebec City

223

Bic National Park

ABOVE: St-Viateur Bagel shop in the Mile End

LEFT: Old Montreal

227

Old Port of Montreal on the St. Lawrence River

New Brunswick

ABOVE: New Brunswick lobster feed

LEFT: Seal Cove, Grand Manan Island

ABOVE: High tide at Hopewell Rocks, Bay of Fundy

LEFT: Low tide at Hopewell Rocks, Bay of Fundy

ABOVE: New Brunswick blueberry field
RIGHT: Hartland Bridge, Saint John River

HARTLAND
NEW
BRUNSWICK

WELCOME
YOU ARE NOW ENTERING THE LONGEST
COVERED BRIDGE IN THE WORLD
1282 FEET

MAXIMUM
10 t

Saint John City Market

ABOVE: St. George Gorge at First Falls

RIGHT: Harbor seals in St. Andrews by-the-Sea

ABOVE: Atlantic Balloon Fiesta, Sussex

LEFT: World's Largest Axe, Nackawic

ABOVE: Alma, Bay of Fundy

LEFT: St. Martins Sea Caves, Bay of Fundy

Prince Edward Island

ABOVE: Teacup Rock, Thunder Cove Beach

LEFT: St. Patrick's Road, New Glasgow

ABOVE: Kayaker in Winter River

LEFT: Paddle boarder at Darnley Basin Beach

ABOVE: Charlottetown

RIGHT: Bellevue Cove

ABOVE: Seal pup on the Gulf of St. Lawrence

LEFT: Great blue heron in Covehead Bay

Confederation Bridge, Marine Rail Historical Park

ABOVE: Potato field and view of the Confederation Bridge in Cape Traverse

LEFT: Greenwich National Park

ABOVE & RIGHT: Green Gables Heritage Place, Prince Edward Island National Park, Cavendish

ABOVE: Confederation Landing Park, Charlottetown

RIGHT: Brighton

Nova Scotia

ABOVE & LEFT: Fortress of Louisbourg

Peggy's Point Lighthouse, Peggy's Cove

ABOVE: Annapolis County

LEFT: Sable River

Mahone Bay

ABOVE: Agricola Street, Halifax

RIGHT: Blue Rocks

Lunenburg waterfront

ABOVE: Whale watching in the Bay of Fundy

LEFT: Kayaker at Black Cove

ABOVE: Maritime fiddler

RIGHT: *Theodore Too* tugboat in Halifax Harbour

Halifax waterfront

ABOVE: Northwest Arm, Halifax Harbour

LEFT: Halifax Central Library

ABOVE: Nova Scotia fishing village

RIGHT: Cabot Trail, Cape Breton Island

Newfoundland & Labrador

ABOVE & RIGHT: Nesting colony of Atlantic puffins near Elliston, Newfoundland

Iceberg off Goose Cove, Newfoundland

ABOVE & RIGHT: The Battery, St. John's, Newfoundland

Gros Morne National Park, Newfoundland

ABOVE: Clothesline in Raleigh, Newfoundland

RIGHT: Norris Cove in Bonne Bay, Newfoundland

Tilting, Fogo Island, Newfoundland

ABOVE: L'Anse aux Meadows National Historic Site, Newfoundland

LEFT: Joe Batt's Arm, Fogo Island, Newfoundland

ABOVE: Battle Harbour, Labrador

RIGHT: Pinware River, Labrador

ABOVE: Inukshuks in Labrador

LEFT: Bull moose in northern Newfoundland

Fishing village on White Cape Harbour, Newfoundland

Canada
Copyright © 2019 HarperCollins Publishers Ltd.
All rights reserved.

Published by Collins, an imprint of HarperCollins Publishers Ltd

First edition

All photography courtesy iStockphoto.com except as noted in the
photography credits section on page 312.

HarperCollins books may be purchased for educational, business,
or sales promotional use through our Special Markets Department.

HarperCollins Publishers Ltd
Bay Adelaide Centre, East Tower
22 Adelaide Street West, 41st Floor
Toronto, Ontario, Canada
M5H 4E3

www.harpercollins.ca

Library and Archives Canada Cataloguing in Publication
information is available upon request.

ISBN 978-1-4434-5850-4

Printed and bound in China
PP 10 9 8 7 6 5 4 3 2 1

Photography Credits

Cory Beatty | @corybeatty
Pages 54–55; 249; 260; 274; 284; 288–89

Tony Beck | @always_an_adventure_inc
Pages 108–9; 115; 121; 170; 185; 191; 211

Bloomberg/Getty Images
Page 88

André Brandt | andrebrandt.com
Pages 158; 168–69; 172; 176; 177

Stéphane Caron | @stephanecaron88
Pages 138; 140–41; 142; 143; 144; 145; 152; 210;
212–13; 215; 216; 217; 224–25; 255

Julio Castro Pardo | @juliocastropardo
Page 61

Raymond Gehman/National Geographic Collection/
Getty Images
Page 87

Lowell Georgia/Getty Images
Page 86

Leah A. Horstman | lahorstmanphotography.com
Pages 5; 21; 68; 69; 72–73; 78

Mark Jinks | markjinksphotography.com
Pages 11; 14; 56; 60; 66–67; 110; 111; 114; 180; 181

Lans Photography | @lansphotography
Pages 209; 248; 250; 251; 253; 254; 258; 262; 263

Florian Ledoux | florian-ledoux.com
Pages 128–29; 132; 133; 146–47; 148; 149; 150; 151; 153

Wayne Lynch/Getty Images
Page 89

Leo MacDonald | @leomacdonaldphoto
Pages 178–79; 186; 207; 270; 271; 275; 285

John E. Marriott | wildernessprints.com
Pages 2–3; 4; 6–7; 9; 15; 23; 28–29; 32–33; 36–37; 47;
50; 51; 58–59; 64; 70; 71; 74; 75; 77; 79; 80; 104–5;
106; 117; 118–19; 120; 130; 131; 136; 137; 154–55;
156–57; 171; 290; 291; 292–93; 308–9

Christopher Martin | christophermartinphotography.com
Pages 16; 30; 31; 57; 214

Anna Mawdsley | @brixtonphotog
Pages 159; 160; 161

Paul Nicklen/National Geographic Collection/Getty Images
Page 17

RyersonClark/Getty Images
Page 90

Nina Stavlund | alwaysanadventure.ca
Pages 184; 188; 189; 192–93; 230–31; 232

Andrea van Ogtrop | vanogtropphotography.com
Page 198

Don Wilson | @wilson.images
Pages 84–85; 116

The following images are not provided with a caption on the pages on which they appear.

Page iii: Moraine Lake in the Valley of the Ten Peaks, Banff National Park

Page iv: Canada geese on Lake Ontario

Page vi: Earl Marriott Secondary/Semiahmoo First Nation Pow Wow in White Rock

Pages 2–3: Mount Assiniboine Provincial Park

Pages 32–33: Tombstone Territorial Park

Pages 54–55: Vermilion Lakes, Banff National Park

Pages 82–83: Aerial view from a seaplane of Nahanni National Park Reserve

Pages 104–5: Wheat field near Leader

Pages 128–29: Fjords east of Baffin Island

Pages 156–57: Hudson Bay Lowlands, Churchill

Pages 178–79: Sauble Beach

Pages 204–5: Percé Rock, Gaspé Peninsula

Pages 230–31: Swallowtail Lightstation, Grand Manan Island

Pages 246–47: Prince Edward Island mustard field

Pages 264–65: Wild horses on Sable Island

Pages 288–89: Cape Spear Lighthouse National Historic Site

Page 314: North American beaver in Ontario